Yellow Line

Sylvia Olsen was born and raised in Victoria, the capital of British Columbia, on Canada's Pacific coastline. When she was seventeen, she married an Indian, a member of the Tsartlip First Nations. Olsen has raised her four children within the Tsartlip community. She went to university at the age of 35 and obtained a Master's degree in history, specializing in Native/White relations in Canada. She now works in first nations community management and is conducting research with teen parents from the Saanich First Nations to increase the community's support network for young parents.

She has written several books for young readers about life within an Indian community ('White Girl' – 2004, 'Yetsa's Sweater' – 2006, 'Which Way Should I Go?' – 2007), educational problems facing young First Nations children ('No Time to Say Goodbye') and teenage motherhood ('The Girl With a Baby' - 2003, 'Just Ask Us' – 2005).

Sylvia Olsen

Yellow Line

Sylvia Olsen
Yellow Line
Teen Readers, level 3

Illustrations: Jette Svane
Edited by: Philip Hewitt

Series editors: Charlotte Bistrup and Ulla Malmmose

ISBN Denmark: 978-87-23-90728-8
www.easyreaders.eu

Easy Readers
EGMONT

Printed in Denmark

Where I come from, kids are in two groups. White kids on one side, Indians on the other side. The other side of the field, the room, the street, the washrooms – everywhere. We're on one side and they're on the other. They live on one side of the Forks River bridge, and we live on the other 5 side. They hang out in their village, and we hang out in ours. In the city, Indians are called First Nations; out here they've always been called Indians, and we don't change things like that *in a hurry.*

Neither village is very special. Ours is bigger than theirs, 10 but altogether there are less than 500 people. Highway 14 passes through. Fifteen minutes to the west is a small port on the *ocean.* An hour and a half or so to the east is the city. It has the police station, the high school, a post office, a big supermarket and even a McDonald's. It's not really a city, 15 just a small town, but it's better than our *dump* of a village.

Nobody in the city cares about our village. The fact is, hardly anyone even knows that it exists.

When Indian kids are on our side of the bridge, they hang out at the *gas station.* White kids hang out just up the 20 road and on the other side of Ruby's store. They walk on one side of the road, we walk on the other. It's as if there's

---

in a hurry ['hʌri] quickly
ocean ['əʊʃən] very large sea (Atlantic, Pacific etc.)
dump unattractive place
gas station place where motorists can buy fuel (*AE* gas = *BE* petrol)

a *solid* yellow line down the middle. Their side of the bridge is the Indian *reserve*. No white kids go down there.

There's a yellow line on the school bus as well. It divides the front of the bus from the back – us at the back, them
5 at the front. You can't see the line, but everybody knows it's there and no one crosses over. It's just the way it is and always has been. Ninety minutes to school and ninety minutes back, and no one puts their foot in the other *territory*. Except Dune.

10 Twenty minutes into the trip to school, the bus turns a corner and there's Dune. He's walking down the middle of the road. I don't know where he lives. There are no telephone lines or *driveways*, just forests and *clear cuts*. Every morning Dune gets on the bus and sits down right
15 in the middle. Behind them and in front of us. With his black hair, white skin and green eyes, no one can be sure whether he's one of them or one of us. People say that Dune and his mom live in a *shack* down by the *beach*. Some people think he belongs to one of the Indian *guys*. Other
20 people think his dad is one of the men from our side.

All the men in our part of Canada are *loggers* or fishermen – when there is work. Most people are old or unemployed.

---

solid ['sɒlɪd] hard and firm
reserve [rɪ'zɜːv] place where only special people, animals etc. can live
territory ['terɪtəri] land which belongs to a country, group of people etc.
driveway road which leads to a private house
clear cut wide, long space between trees in a forest
shack small building that has not been built very well
beach [biːtʃ] sand or stones between the sea and the land
guy [gaɪ] person
logger worker who cuts down trees

Dad says there used to be a bowling alley, a restaurant and a basketball team in our village. Now it's full of old people and *weirdos* who have come here to get away from the city. The one thing that hasn't changed, Dad says, is that people have always known their place. Indians on one side and whites on the other.

Dad says that he *hates* Indians. Mom says she doesn't. But she didn't grow up in the village like Dad did. She says that in the city, people of different races mix with each other all the time.

"Where I come from," Mom says, "we're all just human *beings*."

That's what she says, but it's not how she acts. Mom's been here long enough to feel the same way as Dad, just not long enough to say it out loud. And when the women in the village started a committee to get a separate school bus for the whites, Mom was the *spokesperson*.

That is what our village is like. Or **was** like. Dad and Mom are much like everyone else. I was the same as them. We all lived by the rule of the yellow line. Us and them. Them and us. It's probably hard to imagine that a village like ours actually exists unless you've lived here. And if you've lived here all your life, like I have, you might still find it hard to believe. But I changed, and maybe our village will change, too.

5

10

15

20

25

---

weirdo ['wɪədəʊ] person with unusual habits, clothes etc.
to hate opposite of 'to love'
being living creature
spokesperson ['spəʊksˌpɜːsən] person who speaks for a whole group

---

7

The bus arrives at Ruby's at 7:05. We get in, walk past the front seats and sit in the back. I put my legs on the seat. Nick and Justin sit opposite me.

    The back *row* is usually reserved for guys in *grade* twelve,
5 but this year there aren't any. So the grade elevens – me, Nick and Justin – can sit there for two years. The row ahead of us belongs to Sherry, the only grade eleven girl and a couple of grade ten girls. Sherry and I have been *neighbors* since we were born. Our parents are friends and
10 we're like brother and sister. Or we were. Because this summer she went to visit her *cousins* in the city. When she came back three weeks later, she was different: *hot* – and too good for me.

---

row [rəʊ] line of seats, houses, people etc.
grade standard; level; year (at school etc.)
neighbor [ˈneɪbə] (*BE* neighbour) person who lives near you
cousin [ˈkʌzən] son or daughter of your uncle or aunt
hot (*here:*) grown up from a girl into a young woman

Sherry is sitting three rows up, one row behind the row of *separation*, next to Millie, her little sister. Two things are wrong with this *scene*. Sherry's not sitting in the row in front of us, where she usually sits. And she never talks to Millie. When I look at her again I can see there's a third thing wrong. She's looking around as if she's expecting someone. The bus drives off and stops at the gas station – the Indian bus stop. They have the same system as we do. Oldest on first and the youngest up front behind the driver. When Steve gets on the bus, I sit up a little because he's the next thing that's unusual this morning. He's a big guy, grade twelve, plays rugby, a little shorter than me, but bigger. At six three, I'm the tallest guy in the school, but Steve is the biggest guy at Rocky View High School. He's forty or fifty pounds heavier than me.

Steve usually gets on the bus as if he's half *asleep* and then falls into the last row of Indian seats. But this morning he's *awake* and all cleaned up like he's going somewhere special. He gives Sherry a look and stops for a moment in the *aisle* as if he's deciding where to sit. I sit up a bit higher in my seat and watch him closely.

Finally Charlie, Steve's younger brother, moves over and Steve sits down in the last row of Indian seats. But he sits so that he's half facing the back of the bus. It's then that I see that he's looking straight at Sherry.

5

10

15

20

25

---

separation [ˌsepəˈreɪʃən] state in which two things are kept away from each other
scene [siːn] picture of a situation
asleep sleeping
awake not sleeping
aisle [aɪl] passage between rows of seats

9

Suddenly I'm ready to jump out of my seat and hit him. I'm ready to go, man. Then I decide to wait until he makes one more move. Then I'll *hammer* him. Steve *deserves* it. He's the kind of guy who doesn't know his place. Most of
5 his friends are *rich* white kids from town. He's the most popular guy in the school. Dad says Steve is the only Indian with that distinction. But on the bus he's stayed in his place up until now.

Soon Sherry turns to the side so she's half facing Steve. I
10 can't believe what I'm seeing. She's smiling at him.

The rules of separation in our village are clear and everyone knows them. The most important is: *Date* your own kind. Mom says that people in the city date anyone they want, no matter what color they are. Not in our
15 village. Dad says there are a few guys who married Indians and live over there. But there are no mixed couples living on our side.

I try to keep an eye on what's going on. "Sherry," I call. I talk normal, like I have something to say to her.
20 She doesn't hear.

"Hey, Sherry," I call again.

She turns around and looks at me as if I'm *interrupting* her. "What?"

"So what's up?" I say, trying to break the link between
25 her and Steve.

---

to hammer to hit very hard
to deserve [dɪ'zɜːv] to have earned something by good or bad actions
rich [rɪtʃ] having lots and lots of money
to date to arrange a meeting with a person of the opposite sex
to interrupt [ˌɪntə'rʌpt] to stop an action before it is complete; to say
  something while another person is speaking

She shakes her head as if she can't hear me. Feeling like an idiot, I *slide* back down into the back seat. Before I *disappear*, Steve sends me a look that seems to say 'What a *moron!*'

I want to jump out of my seat and *beat* him *up*.   5

---

to slide – slid – slid to move slowly and smoothly across a surface
to disappear [ˌdɪsəˈpɪə] to become impossible to see any longer
moron [ˈmɔːrɒn] person of very low intelligence
to beat up – beat – beaten to hit somebody hard many times

CHAPTER TWO

By the time we get to the school, I can hardly sit still.

"Hey, man," says Justin as I push past him. "Are you in some kind of hurry this morning?"

I finally catch up with Sherry at the *parking lot*.

5 "Hey," I say. "What's up?"

"Huh?" Sherry gives me a 'Who-are-you?' look.

"How are you doing?" I try again.

"Fine."

"What are you doing?"

10 "Going to class, *stupid*," she says. She's treating me like an idiot who's trying to make a date with her. She's right, in a way. I've certainly thought about getting my hands on her.

"Yeah. Of course."

15 She runs ahead to Steve.

"Hey," I hear her *silky* voice.

"What's **his** problem?"

My ears are *ringing* like church *bells*, and my feet feel as heavy as *concrete*.

20 My body and mind are *confused*. Sherry and I used to jump off the bus together!

bell

shadow ['ʃædəʊ]

concrete ['kɒŋkriːt]

---

parking lot open space where cars can be parked
stupid ['stjuːpɪd] very silly
silky very soft and smooth
to ring – rang – rung to produce the sound made when metal is hit
confused [kən'fjuːzd] unable to think clearly or react correctly

Justin and Nick catch up with me.

"She's too hot for you now," Nick laughs.

"Yeah," says Justin. "Now even Mr. Basketball *ain't* good enough for her."

That's what I mean. I'm not a nobody – I'm a basketball   5
hero. I'm the captain of the school basketball team, and last year I was the highest *scorer* on the senior team. We were *provincial* champions. And who was the best player? Me – Vince Hardy, Mr. Basketball. And who was at every game *cheering* for me? Sherry Porter.   10

"Shut up, Justin," I say. "Sherry's like my sister, man. I'm just looking out for her."

"Yeeeaaah," says Nick slowly. "Who does Steve think he is?"

"You guys should have seen them when you were asleep in the bus," I say. "Eyes all over each other."   15

"We mustn't let Steve get too close to her," says Justin. "She's the hottest *chick* this year."

Inside the school, Sherry's *leaning* against her *locker*, looking at Steve. Steve is talking to her and smiling at her. Without talking, Nick, Justin and I form a line shoulder   20
to shoulder, me on the locker side. We move forward. As

---

ain't [eɪnt] *(slang:)* isn't; am not

hero [ˈhɪərəʊ] very popular or brave person

scorer person who wins points in a game

provincial [prəˈvɪnʃəl] belonging to a province

to cheer [tʃɪə] to shout in order to show happiness or encouragement

chick (slang:) girl

to lean – leant [lent] *– leant* to rest the side or back of your body against
     something upright

locker small metal cupboard where you can keep personal items safe at school,
     at the gym or at the swimming pool

I walk past Steve, I push him against the locker. He turns round quickly and *grabs* me with both hands. A crowd quickly forms in the hall. Nick and Justin, like the *wimps* that they are, hurry away down the hall. I'm left hanging
5 from Steve's arms.

"Vince," Sherry says, "you used to be so cool."

Steve drops me like a hot potato. While he was holding on, I was *scared*, but once I'm free I start shouting at him.

"Get your hands off me," I shout in his face.

10 "If you know what's good for you, you'll leave me alone," says Steve quietly. Then he turns to Sherry and says, "Don't worry about him."

What's going on? Since when does he need to tell her not to worry about me?

15 Nick and Justin come back now that Steve and the crowd have gone.

"Hey, Vince," says a voice.

I look round. The little Indian chick who follows Steve around is still standing where the crowd was.

20 "It happens," she says. "Don't worry about it."

---

to grab to catch something with a quick movement of the hand
wimp person without a strong character
scared [skeəd] worried or nervous about something

CHAPTER THREE

"Pass!" I shout.

The basketball season starts in two weeks and our team is no good. All the good players except me *graduated* last year.

"Vince!" shouts *Coach* Baker. I go over to talk to him. "You're the leader this year," he says. "We need more than baskets. We need *motivation*. What's wrong with you today?"

"Vinny. Vinny." Girls' voices interrupt Coach Baker. Charlie and some of the guys from the reserve are standing at the *gym* door. "We're counting on you, Vinny. You're our man."

A girl shouts, "Hey, white boy, you sure got *hairy* legs."

"Vince, keep your eye on the ball," Coach Baker shouts.

"Look at his *spider* legs," the girl shouts again. "He looks like he just *crawled* out of a hole in the wall."

"Vince," calls Nick. "Where's your game, man?"

I shake my head. The only thing I can think about are the *taunts* coming from the door of the gym.

---

to graduate [ˈɡrædʒueɪt] to finish your education at High School *(AE)* or university *(BE)*
coach [kəʊtʃ] trainer of a sports team
motivation [ˌməʊtɪˈveɪʃən] strong wish to do something without the need to be told
gym [dʒɪm] sports hall
hairy covered with hair
spider [ˈspaɪdə] small creature with eight thin legs
crawl [krɔːl] to walk on hands and knees
taunt [tɔːnt] unkind remark intended to make somebody angry or unhappy

"Looks like he's *gonna* break," someone says, and the others begin to *giggle*.

I turn quickly round to get a better look at them – too quickly. I fall and hit my face against the wall. Now they start laughing as if they've just seen the funniest thing in the world. ₅

"Hey," Coach Baker finally shouts at the crowd. "Either get changed or get out of the gym."

"Losers!" I shout as they start pushing their way out of the door. "Shut your *freaking* mouths and get out of here!"

Suddenly they stop and start walking back into the gym. ₁₀

"You gonna throw us out, white boy?" Charlie shouts. "Come on. Let's see you try."

They form a *semicircle* around me. Out of the corner of my eye I see two big guys moving toward me. Coach Baker grabs my shirt and pulls me away from them, ₁₅

"I told you guys to get out of here," he shouts. "I don't want to see you in the gym again unless you want to play."

"Later," shouts Charlie. "We'll get you later, Hardy."

"Later," I shout as he leaves. "I'll be there."

"*Chicken*," a girl shouts. "He's got chicken legs with black ₂₀ hairs! *Yuck!*"

"*Settle down*, Vince," says Coach Baker, pushing me down on a *bench*. "Listen to me, boy. If I catch you fighting

---

gonna (AE) going to
to giggle to laugh in a silly way
freaking this word is used to replace a rude word beginning with 'f…'
semicircle ['semɪsɜːkl] half a circle
chicken ['tʃɪkən] farm bird which lays eggs and is good to eat
yuck! [jʌk] word which expresses strong dislike
to settle down to relax; to become calm and quiet
bench long seat without a back

17

those guys anywhere near this school, you'll be out of the team. I don't care how many baskets you get. There are no fighters in this team."

"Chicken legs!" I can still hear the girl.

5 I sit on the edge of the bench and feel real anger. I feel like I want to break a few heads.

Chicken legs.

The words *scream* around in my head. My head hurts where I hit it on the wall. Losers. They're all losers.

10 Suddenly I look down at my legs. They're long and white and covered in thick black hairs. They shock me. I mean, they're so *ugly* I feel *sick*.

"Tomorrow, Coach," I shout. "I'm finished today."

I race out of the gym.

---

to scream to make a loud sound when you are in pain or danger
ugly [ˈʌgli] opposite of 'beautiful'
sick unwell

CHAPTER FOUR

When I get on the bus after school, I feel *terrible*. Not just
terrible but *terrified*. That's how you feel when a gang of
tough guys promises to beat you up.

"Keep looking over your shoulder, white boy," says one
massive guy. "We're ready to beat the *crap* out of you."   5

Charlie puts his foot out as if he wants to *trip* me and
says, "Better keep your eyes open, white boy."

"Good thing you've got your *pants* on," says an Indian
girl as I pass. "I'd cover up too if my legs looked like yours."

I'm just going to tell her how ugly she is when I notice   10
she's sitting next to the girl who talked to me in the hall.
Our eyes meet. She smiles as if to say 'I don't think they're
very funny, either'.

I keep my mouth shut. Walk past and fall into the back
seat.   15

"We can take those guys," says Nick.

"Yeah. We'll get them at the gas station," shouts Justin
to Manny and Turner, who are sitting a few seats in front
of us. "You guys want to meet us at the gas station? We're
going to teach those morons a lesson."   20

Manny and Turner won't be any help. They're brothers

---

terrible ['terɪbl] very bad
terrified very worried; full of fear
tough [tʌf] physically or mentally strong
crap rubbish; shit
to trip to make a person fall by holding out your foot
pants (AE) trousers

and both in grade eight. But they've been in grade eight for a couple of years, so they could be older than me. "Shut up, Justin," I say. "I'm not fighting anyone."

"What? You're going to let them treat you like that?"
5 asks Nick.

"No," I say. But I'm thinking 'yes'. I'm a wimp with chicken legs. Those guys would kill me. And Nick and Justin are as *skinny* as me. None of us have ever been in a real fight. We've pushed a few guys around a bit, that's all.
10 This could turn into something big.

"We'll get them," I *mumble*. "Just not right now."

I slide down into my seat and try to disappear.

After a few minutes, I raise my head and take a look at Steve and Sherry. Steve's in his usual seat and Sherry's two
15 rows behind. Both are sitting *sideways*, facing each other and smiling and talking. They're *sticking to* the seating rules, but Sherry's acting like Steve's her boyfriend. The worst thing is she looks like she doesn't think there's anything wrong with it.
20 Charlie is sitting on the seat next to Steve. He's looking my way.

"Vinny!" he shouts. "He's our man. Maybe today, maybe tomorrow. We're coming after you. You are going to be one very sorry little white boy."
25 I want to ignore everyone, but I keep looking at the girl who talked to me at school. She's turned slightly my way. I get the feeling she's looking at me, too. I try to ignore her,

---

skinny physically thin
to mumble [ˈmʌmbl] to say something quietly and unclearly
sideways pointing to one side
to stick to – stuck [stʌk] *– stuck* to keep to a rule or regulation

——
20

but next time I look, she smiles at me. There's no doubt about it. She has big white teeth and full red lips. She's wearing the kind of *lipstick* that makes you want to eat her lips. She looks soft and *friendly* when she smiles, not like anyone else on the bus.

I quickly look away in case she starts to giggle with the rest of the girls. Why is she being friendly? The next time our eyes meet, I smile back. Am I *crazy*? What am I doing? I sit back into the seat and close my eyes. But I can't get my mind off her lips and her eyes. I can still see her smile.

She's an Indian. Mom and Dad would go crazy if they knew what I was thinking. What difference does it make anyway? When Charlie and his gang get me I'll be dead. My eyes stay closed until the bus stops at the Indian bus stop.

"Later, Vinny," I hear Charlie shout.

"Sometime," says another voice. "You'll never know when."

"Chicken legs," I hear through the mass of voices and giggles.

The bus door closes. I sit up. Steve is the only Indian left on the bus. He doesn't get off. He moves into the seat where Dune had been sitting. He is directly in front of Sherry. They are talking softly. She can have him. They deserve each other. Go for it, Steve! Wait until I tell my parents and they tell Sherry's. They'll take care of you, big guy. But then I realize that I don't care about any of that

---

friendly behaving like a friend
crazy [ˈkreɪzi] stupid

lipstick

---

anymore. It's not about Steve and Sherry. It's about Charlie and his gang who are going to kill me. And worse than that. I can't stop thinking about the girls staring at me and giggling.

5 Chicken. Chicken legs.

What's wrong with me?

Then I notice the Indian girl from the hall is still sitting in her seat. Why didn't she get off at the Indian bus stop? She walks off with Steve when the bus stops at Ruby's and
10 waits next to the bus stop until I get off.

"Don't worry about those guys, Vince," she says. "They're morons."

Then she smiles at me again and I *melt*.

"Hey, Sweetie!" calls Nick. "Are you waiting for me?"

15 "Shut up," she says. Then she turns to me. "My name's Raedawn. I'm Steve's cousin."

"Ooohhh," says Justin. "Steve's cousin. Tell Steve he'd better watch out because we're after him."

"Get out of here, Justin," I say.

20 The girl smiles again and turns away.

"She's a nice piece," says Justin. "Even if she does live over the bridge."

"Shut up, you *pig*!" I shout. "Just shut up."

It's not only Nick and Justin I want to shut up. I want the
25 whole world to shut up. I want everything to slow down so I can work out what's happening to me. I run all the way home.

---

to melt to turn from a solid to a liquid state (e.g. ice to water)
pig farm animal from which we get pork and bacon

Since Ronny, my older brother, moved away three years ago, *meals* at our house are *boring*. Mom puts the food on the table. Dad sits at one end. Mom at the other. I sit between them facing the wall. I keep my head down, eat and get out of the kitchen as fast as I can. Mom and Dad 5 talk about *logging*, Dad's boss, Mom's friends or who said what to who. It's always the same *stuff*. Nothing much happens in our town, and if something does happen, the whole town knows the details in a matter of minutes.

I sit down at the dinner table and Mom says, "Vince, I 10 hear there was some trouble on the bus today."

I've been home for less than an hour and she already knows everything.

"Huh?" I *pretend* I don't know what she's talking about.

"I hear the Indian boys were *threatening* you," she says. 15

"What's that?" asks Dad.

"Nora phoned and said she heard Justin and Nick saying that the Indian boys are after Vince."

"No way," says Dad. "Those Indians better keep their hands off my boy." 20

"And Vince did nothing to *provoke* them," says Mom.

---

meal [miːl] breakfast, lunch and supper are *meals*
boring [ˈbɔːrɪŋ] not interesting
logging cutting down trees etc.
stuff [stʌf] material or topic
to pretend [prɪˈtend] to say, think or do something that is not true
to threaten [ˈθretn] to say that you will do something bad
to provoke [prəˈvəʊk] *somebody* to give somebody a reason to react

They keep on talking as if I'm not in the room. "Of course he didn't. I've told Vince since he was a kid to stay away from the Indians," says Dad.

"And they said something about Sherry and one of the Indian boys," says Mom.

Now Dad turns to me: "What's she talking about?"

"You know Steve. I told you about him. He's the rugby player, the one who was *voted* the most popular guy in the school."

"Yeah, I remember," says Dad. "So what?"

If I tell them about Sherry and Steve, maybe they won't want to know what happened to me on the bus. "Well," I continue, "they're getting very friendly."

"What do you mean 'getting very friendly'?" asks Dad angrily. "Are you telling me some Indian guy is getting interested in Donnie's little girl?"

"Poor Sherry," says Mom. "She needs to be careful."

"So what are you doing about it?" asks Dad, like this is suddenly my problem.

"Me?" I say. "What can I do about it?"

"If some Indian is after Sherry, you better make sure he doesn't get his hands on her."

"Who says Sherry doesn't like it?" I ask.

"What did you say?" says Dad. He puts down his *fork* and points his finger at me. "Sherry doesn't like it, son. I know Sherry doesn't like it. She's the daughter of Donnie and Deb. That girl has been brought up the right way. She knows to stick to her own."

to vote to give your official support to
  a political party, individual etc.

fork [fɔːk]

"Is that the problem you had on the bus?" asks Mum.

"I don't want to talk about it," I say.

Mom and Dad don't understand one thing about me. I can talk to them, but they don't listen.

"You better talk about it, son," says Dad. "No girl of 5
Donnie's is going around with a *damn* Indian. She's been looking grown up lately, and now they're following her around like a *pack* of dogs."

I pick up my plate of spaghetti and go down the *stairs* to my room in the *basement*. 10

"Vince," calls Mom. "You need to talk to us. We can help."

I shut the door.

Before Mom finishes her spaghetti, she'll be on the phone with Deb, Sherry's mom, telling everything. Dad will be going next door to tell Donnie his version. With some 15
satisfaction I think that will be the end of Sherry and Steve.

★

The next day, Sherry arrives late at the bus stop.

"You loser, Vince," she *snaps* at me. "You think you can *ruin* what me and Steve have by telling your mom and dad? I don't care what anyone says," she says as she gets on the 20
bus. "I'm with Steve. Get used to it!"

At the next stop, Steve gets on and walks straight down the aisle and through the dividing line. He sits down next

---

damn [dæm] word that is used to give extra force to a statement
pack group of dogs, wolves etc.
stairs [steəz] row of steps in a house from one floor to another
basement ['beɪsmənt] rooms of a house below the ground floor
satisfaction [ˌsætɪsˈfækʃn] feeling of happiness about the result of an action
to snap [snæp] to say something in a sharp, angry voice
to ruin ['ruːɪn] to spoil or destroy completely

to Sherry. In one move, he *blows away* years of school bus seating arrangements.

But the real reason why I'm so angry is because Sherry's treating me like a moron. Nobody else on the bus cares where they sit, either. Charlie and the other Indians don't seem to notice. The bus drives off, then suddenly stops again and the door opens.

"Hurry up, Raedawn," says Alice, the bus driver. "You aren't usually late."

"Sorry," says Raedawn. "I had to print something out on my computer and it took longer than usual."

There is a strange feeling in my *stomach* when I hear her voice. She sits down on her usual seat, then turns round to look at me. She gives me a little *wave* and then faces the front of the bus.

"Did you see that?" asks Nick. "That chick thinks you're *cute*, Vinny. She's waving to you."

"Say hello to the little girl, Vinny," shouts Justin, loud enough for everyone to hear.

I want to *punch* him in the face. I want her to know that I think he's an idiot. I want to ask her where she got a cool name like Raedawn. Then I remember she's not one of us. I sit back and think about her lips and her smile. Something has gone seriously wrong with me. Why can't I get her out of my head?

"They all want you, Vince," laughs Nick. "The guys want to kill you and the girls want your legs – they love them!"

"Shut up," I say. "Just shut up!"

---

to blow [bləʊ] *away – blew* [bluː] *– blown* to make something disappear
stomach [ˈstʌmək] organ of the body which starts to process the food you eat
wave movement of the hand in greeting or farewell
cute [kjuːt] very pretty, handsome or attractive
to punch [pʌntʃ] to hit with your fist, like a boxer

If troubles come in threes, my troubles should soon be over. *Threats* from Charlie and the gang, *insults* from the girls, stupid tough-guy stuff from Nick and Justin, *lovey-dovey* from Sherry and Steve, and Mom and Dad are talking to the whole village. Steve and Sherry are the biggest news in a   5 long time. Then there's Raedawn, who watches me like she's *hunting*. She quietly keeps her eyes on me. When she says 'Hi', I get a funny feeling in my stomach. When she's not around, I think about her eyes and her lips and that's not all.

On the bus on Friday afternoon, I keep my head down.   10 Maybe I can get through the weekend without all hell breaking loose.

"Vinny, how about tonight? At the river? Under the bridge. Be there!" It's Charlie.

The bus stops and the Indians start to get off.   15

"If you're not there, Vinny," Charlie goes on, "we'll come and find you, and it'll be worse."

"Leave him alone, Charlie," says Steve.

"Hey, man," says Charlie. "This ain't got nothing to do with you, *Bro*. This is between him and me."   20

"No, it's not," Steve says. "It's about me and Sherry. So leave it alone."

---

threat [θret] statement that you are going to hurt somebody
insult [ˈɪnsʌlt] rude statement that is intended to hurt
lovey-dovey [ˌlʌviˈdʌvi] very romantic behaviour
to hunt [hʌnt] to follow an person or animal in the hope of catching it
Bro [brəʊ] short for 'brother'

Charlie stands up next to Steve. He's a head shorter, but powerfully built. "You can have your white chick. But this idiot's not going to push us around. That's my business."

Steve sits down and says, "Leave him alone, Charlie."

5 "Tonight." Charlie ignores Steve and shouts, "Be there or else, Vinny. Eight thirty."

"We'll be there," says Nick.

"We're ready for you morons," says Justin.

"Shut up!" I say. "They're not after you guys."

10 The bus moves off with Steve and Raedawn still in their seats. She's waiting when I get off the bus.

"Don't go down to the river," she says. "Stay home. They won't come looking for you if you stay in your village."

"We're not afraid of those morons," says Justin. "We'll

15 be there."

She ignores him, looks me in the eye and says, "I mean it, Vince. Don't go down there." And to Justin she says, "You're a bit of a moron yourself. And if you know what's good for you, you'll stay at home, too."

20 He moves toward her and I pull him back.

"Come on," I say. "Leave her alone."

"What's with you these days, Vince?" asks Nick. "Does that girl have something on you? You're acting like a loser."

Raedawn disappears.

*

25 At six thirty, Justin and Nick *bang* on the basement door. They push past me into my room.

"Hey, man, we got a bottle of whiskey from Nick's

---

to bang [bæŋ] to make a sudden loud noise by hitting something

---

place," says Justin. He opens the bottle and takes a drink. "Have some, Vince. You're going to need it tonight."

I hold up my hand and say, "I pass, man. I'm not going tonight."

⁵ "You can't not go. They'll come looking for you," says Nick.

"Then they'll have to find me here. I'm not going," I say. I surprise myself by how sure I am. If this had happened a few weeks ago I would have drunk the whiskey and a few beers and been waiting at the river for those idiots. I would ¹⁰ have made sure all the white boys in the village were there, too. But that was before I became a weakling. It wasn't Charlie's threats that changed everything. It was those girls and all their stupid comments. 'Chicken legs, you need to be *plucked*'. Forget being Mr. Basketball. I'm a real *coward*.

¹⁵ That's not all that's changed. I don't care about Steve and Sherry like I used to. The new, grown-up Sherry looks good, but she's a *bitch*. I feel sorry for Steve. He's got himself into a terrible *mess*, and he doesn't know it yet. Another thing is Raedawn. When I'm not worrying about ²⁰ getting killed, I'm thinking about her. If she's going to be down at the river, I don't want to be beaten up in front of her. I'd rather be called a wimp.

Nick grabs my *jacket* and throws it at me.

"Come on, let's go," he says. "If we get there early we ²⁵ can work out a strategy."

"I said I'm not going.
We aren't going to win, guys.

to pluck [plʌk] to pull out hairs or feathers
coward [ˈkaʊəd] person who has no courage
bitch woman of bad character
mess situation where everything is out of place

jacket [ˈdʒækɪt]

There will be at least ten of them and only three of us."

"What's with you, man?" asks Justin. "You're the basketball star. Since when have a *bunch* of Indians worried you?"

"Since I don't want to get killed."

"We can take them, man," says Nick. "Let's go down there and work out a strategy. They'll arrive half *drunk* and we'll be ready for them."

"Forget it," I say. "You're already half drunk yourself. And they play rugby – we play basketball. Strategy isn't going to help us tonight."

"You sure?" asks Nick as he passes the now almost empty whiskey bottle back to Justin.

"Yeah, I'm sure." And the drunker they get, the surer I become.

Justin gets off the bed and leans against the wall. "No problem, Vinny. We'll take care of them."

When they finally *stagger* out of my room, I lock the basement door behind them. I realize that I used to be that stupid.

The house feels empty. I run upstairs, lock the front door and close the windows. When I get back to my room I lock the windows and fall on my bed. I start playing a video game. My plan is to concentrate on the game and forget everything else.

It works. Soon the only thing left in my head is Raedawn. I can see her hiding behind the *bushes* near the bridge. She's probably waiting to see if I'm stupid enough to show up.

---

bunch [bʌntʃ] group of people
drunk [drʌŋk] having drunk too much alcohol
to stagger [ˈstæɡə] to walk unsteadily after having been hurt or having drunk too much
bush [bʊʃ] large plant like a small tree

31

CHAPTER SEVEN

"Vince! Vince!"

Someone is banging on the basement door. I jump off my bed. They're here. They're going to kill me.

"Vince!" there is *panic* in the voice. "Open the door, you
5 idiot. Let us in."

It's Nick and Justin. Charlie and the gang are probably right behind them. But when I open the door, Nick and Justin are alone. They push their way into my room and both start talking at once.

10 "We were good tonight, man," says Nick. "You should have seen us."

I look at them quickly, but there are no signs that they've been fighting.

"What are you talking about, man?" I ask.

15 "Here's the story, man," says Nick. "It was so right! You tell it, Justin."

So Justin says, "We were down there waiting under the bridge in a safe place, so we could work out our strategy." Then he stops. "You tell it, Nick," he says.

20 "What's with you guys?" I ask. "Just tell me what happened."

Nick suddenly sounds *sober*. "Like Justin said, we're behind a bush when three cars arrive. There must have been eight or ten guys and a few girls. They're all smoking *joints*. They're

---

panic ['pænɪk] sudden strong feeling of fear
sober ['səʊbə] opposite of 'drunk'
joint [dʒɔɪnt] cigarette containing the drug cannabis

laughing. Charlie shouts your name a few times and the girls were laughing and talking about plucking your legs."

"All right, Nick," I say. "I don't care what they think of my legs. What happened?"

Nick's thinking hard. "Well, they'd only been there a few minutes when Steve arrives with Sherry. He tells them to go home and forget it. And after a while they all get back into their cars and disappear." 5

"And?" I ask. He hasn't told me everything. "What else?"

"Nothing." 10

"That's not why you were laughing."

"No," he says. "The real story happened after that. Go ahead, Justin. I told the first part. You tell the rest."

Justin giggles like a girl. "So we come out of the bushes and *bump into* the chick that's always looking at you." 15

"Raedawn," says Nick.

"Yeah," says Justin. "She was in the bushes quite near us all the time. So there she is, looking just as cute as ever. She even gives us one of those sexy looks and says 'Hey, guys, what are you doing tonight?' Just like that. You should have heard her. It was like she was giving it away. Right, Nick?" 20

Nick says nothing. He is lying on his stomach with his head in his hands. But I am very angry.

"What are you saying? What was she giving away?"

Justin laughs. "She was giving it all away. Everything, man. She wanted us." He looks over at Nick. "What are we supposed to do? We didn't want to *disappoint* her." 25

Suddenly Justin gets serious and says. "Then just when

---

to bump into somebody to meet somebody by chance
to disappoint [ˌdɪsəˈpɔɪnt] *somebody* to not fulfil somebody's wishes

———
33

we're ready, she starts pulling away. She starts shouting at us, telling us to get off her. But we got some right, both of us. Nick first and then me. You should have been there, buddy. You could have had some, too."

5   I start shaking. "Get out of here!" I shout.

"What's wrong with you?" asks Nick as he stands up.

"Yeah, Vince," says Justin. "We got some tonight. She'd give it to anyone. No big deal."

"Get out of here!" I scream. "Get out of my house!"

10   I'm ready to *explode*. They finally stagger out of the basement. When they're gone, I put my shoes and jacket on and race toward the bridge. Whenever I hear a car coming up the road or behind me, I hide in the bushes.

"Where are you, Raedawn?" I shout when I reach the
15 bridge. "Raedawn, can you hear me?" I shout in both directions – up the river and down toward the ocean.

I stop and listen. There is no answer. Only the sound of blood *pounding* in my head. I run across the bridge and come to the place that Nick and Justin described. It is a
20 small *clearing* in the bushes. Raedawn was here. This is where it happened. I'm so angry I could kill.

I go back onto the bridge. I'm too *wound up* to go home. I walk through the woods to the beach. When the woods open up onto the sand, the sky is bright but *clouds* cover
25 the moon and stars. The beach stretches away into the distance. I feel cold in the *breeze* from the ocean. I put my

---

to explode [ɪksˈpləʊd] to break into small pieces with a loud bang
to pound to beat very strongly
clearing place in a wood where no trees are growing
wound [waʊnd] *up* emotionally worried
cloud [klaʊd] mass of water vapour in the air
breeze light wind

3*

jacket on and wait. Slowly the moon appears from behind the clouds. A line of light from the moon *stretches* across the water to my feet. It's like a *pathway* to God. I can't move. For a moment, I think God is calling me. I'm ready to start making promises to Him, but something tells me that God would not want to talk to me.

I'm disappointed that I don't have some time with God, but suddenly the clouds close together again, shutting out the moon. I start walking back home, leaving all thoughts of God on the beach.

*

The lights are on when I get home. Mom and Dad are listening to country music in the living room. I need to speak to someone. I even think about going upstairs and talking to Mom and Dad. What would I say to them? They wouldn't understand what I'm going through. Dad would be angry that I had not wanted to fight Charlie. He'd tell me about how he took on a whole gang of Indians with one hand tied behind his back when he was my age. Mom would have something positive to say. And if I told them I was worried about what happened to Raedawn? Forget it.

She didn't ask for it. She didn't want them. She couldn't have wanted them.

---

to stretch (here:) to cover a certain distance
pathway [ˈpɑːθweɪ] road for walking along

Dad's watching golf on TV when I go upstairs in the morning. Mom's making breakfast in the kitchen.

"You see Sherry last night?" Dad asks.

"No."

"Do you know where she was last night?" asks Mom.   5

"Why should I know where Sherry is?" I ask.

"You and Sherry used to be *inseparable*," she says. "This is a small town. There can't be too many places she could have been."

Dad *switches* off the TV in the living room. This doesn't   10
often happen, so I know it's serious. "Vince, get in here. I need to talk to you."

"What?"

"Where were you last night?"

"Playing video games downstairs."   15

"Where were Justin and Nick?"

"How should I know?"

"Because you and Nick and Justin have spent every Friday night together since you were able to walk."

"Except last night, okay? What's the big deal?"   20

I'm getting *annoyed*. Why doesn't he get to the point?

"You want to know the big deal? Sherry didn't get home until 2 AM last night. She staggered in through her

---

inseparable [ɪnˈsepərəbl] not able to be kept apart
to switch to connect or disconnect a piece of electric equipment
annoyed [əˈnɔɪd] slightly angry

bedroom window *glassy eyed* and *smelling* of *marijuana*."

"Since when is Sherry my problem?" I say. "She doesn't even look at me anymore."

"She said she was with you and Justin and Nick." Dad's
5 eyes are looking for a sign that I've been smoking *pot*.

"So why didn't you come downstairs last night? You could have seen for yourself that I wasn't *stoned*."

"You weren't home when we first checked," shouts Mom from the kitchen. "And by 2 AM your father was too
10 angry and had had a few drinks. I made him promise to sleep it off before he talked to you. I didn't want a *row*."

"Well, there wouldn't have been a row. I was home all night except for a few minutes when I went out for a walk. I wasn't drinking or smoking. I don't know what the others
15 were doing last night and I don't care."

"Vince," Mom asks. "You seem worried. Is there anything you want to talk about?"

Yeah, I want to tell you that I'm going to get killed by a gang of Indians, that I feel like a chicken because a bunch
20 of girls keep *teasing* me. I think I'm falling in love with an Indian girl I've never really met.

What? I think I'm falling in love with Raedawn? I'm not. She's been with Nick **and** Justin. "I don't want to talk about

---

glassy eyed [ˌglɑːsiˈaɪd] having eyes that show little or no expression
to smell – smelt – smelt to give out or register an aroma
marijuana [ˌmærɪˈwɑːnə] illegal drug made from the leaves of the hemp plant
pot (slang:) marijuana
stoned (slang:) feeling relaxed or excited after taking drugs
row [raʊ] argument
to tease [tiːz] to make jokes about a person's looks, character etc.

anything, Mom," I say, but this is a lie. I *desperately* want to talk to someone before I go *mad*, but that person is not my Mom.

Dad gets up off the sofa. He still smells of beer. "Let me tell you, Vince," he says. "If Sherry's still hanging out with 5 that Indian, Donnie's going to send her into town to live with his sister."

"Sherry can hang out with whoever she wants," I say.

"What did you say?" Dad moves closer to me.

"I said 'mind your own business'." Suddenly I'm on 10 Sherry's side. "If she wants to hang out with Steve, that's up to her."

"Who is this Steve?" Dad shouts. "Some useless Indian who sits around smoking pot? I'm shocked to hear that from you, Vince. I raised you different from that." 15

"Vince," says Mom, "of course we can be friends with everybody, but you know how Donnie and Deb feel about Sherry having an Indian boyfriend."

"Of course I know how they feel. I know how you guys feel as well." I race downstairs and *slam* my bedroom door. 20

---

desperate [ˈdespərət] willing to do anything to improve a bad situation
mad crazy
to slam to close with a loud bang

I spend all Saturday in my room playing video games. On Sunday, when Justin phones, I tell him I'm sick.

I'm not exactly lying. I don't want to listen to anyone, to see anyone or think about anything. I don't even want
5 to *breathe*. Yeah, I'm sick – sick of the whole damn world. I switch off the light and just lie on the bed. I turn the music up loud. Maybe it will help me stop thinking about Raedawn and my plans to hit Nick's and Justin's heads together.

10 Someone is *knocking* on the back door. Damn those guys. Don't they know that I don't want to see them? But the knocking doesn't stop. "Who is it?" I shout.

"It's me," a girl's voice says. "Open the door."

"Who's 'me'?" I ask. What girl would be knocking on my
15 door on a Sunday evening? Or ever?

"Sherry. It's Sherry. Let me in."

I open the door. She looks as if she's waiting for me to explode.

"Don't just stand there," I say. "Come in."

20 I want to shout at her but, at the same time, I want to *hug* her and tell her how much I've *missed* her.

"Do you mind?" she asks.

"Do I mind what?"

---

to breathe [briːð] to take air into your body
to knock [nɒk] to hit
to hug [hʌg] to hold somebody hard in your arms to show that you love them
to miss *(here:)* to feel unhappy that a thing or a person is no longer there

"Is it okay that I'm over here?"

She takes one step into the room and then stops.

"Sit down," I say and point to her *favorite* chair.

"Vinny…" she begins as she sits down. Then she starts to cry. "I need to talk to you. You must help me." 5

"So you're here because you need my help?" I ask her.

"No, Vinny. I'm here because you're my best friend in the whole world and I miss you and I need you. Friends need each other. Even if one of them has been acting badly."

"Yeah," I say. "You got that right." 10

"I know, I know. And I am so sorry."

Suddenly I realize how much I've missed her. She's the person I've needed to talk to.

She says she's in trouble with her mom and dad. They caught her *kissing* Steve goodnight and were waiting in her 15 bedroom when she climbed in the window. Now they've decided to send her to the city to live with her aunt and uncle next week. Until then she's *grounded*. No Steve, no friends and maybe even no school.

By now she's crying *hysterically*. I don't want to shout 20 at her any more. I want to hold her. But when I finally get my arms around her, a strange thing happens. She's not hot Sherry any more. She's next-door Sherry with makeup running down her face.

"Vinny, Vinny," she cries. "You have to help me." 25

---

favorite ['feɪvrət] (BE favourite) thing or person that you like most

to kiss to touch a person emotionally with your lips

to ground somebody to punish a young person by not allowing them to go out in their free time

hysterical [hɪ'sterɪkl] showing strong uncontrolled emotion

41

I feel *guilty*. This whole mess is my *fault*. My mom and dad told her mom and dad what I said. I did not want to get her into trouble. I never thought it would lead to this.

I try to think of something *brilliant* to do.

5 "I love Steve." Sherry's quieter now. "And I love you like a brother. What am I going to do if I have to go away? We've been together since we were born!"

"I thought you'd forgotten about me."

"I'm so sorry, Vinny. I was such a *fool*. I started thinking
10 I was something that I wasn't. Guys were looking at me in a way they'd never looked before. I thought I was too good for you – for everybody in fact. You were the only guy who *reminded* me of who I really was."

"It's okay, Sherry," I say. "We're going to have to talk to
15 our parents. You can't move to town, Sherry. I would miss you. That would be crap."

"What's crap is all that talk about sticking to your own and Indians being drunk and stoned and no good for us. Steve's the best thing in my life. He's the one who told the
20 others not to beat you up. He's the one who tells me to do my homework and respect my parents. He's the one who says I shouldn't drink too much."

"Your parents would never believe that," I say.

"Then we've got to make them. And quickly."

25 "I'll think of something."

---

guilty ['gɪlti] responsible for a crime of something bad
it's my fault [fɒlt] I am responsible for something bad happening
brilliant ['brɪljənt] extremely good
fool silly person; idiot
to remind [rɪ'maɪnd] *somebody* to tell somebody something they may have
   forgotten

I still feel responsible for her problem, so I tell her I'll talk to my parents.

I know that won't do any good. My parents are worse than hers when it comes to *prejudice*. What I really have in my mind is Raedawn, and I want to talk to Sherry about her.

"I've got to get home, Vinny. We'll talk later. Thank you. Thank you."

She gets up to leave but turns round at the door. "Vinny, I haven't told Steve that I'm moving."

"You have to."

"Not yet. We must think of something to change my parents' minds. Then I won't have to tell him at all."

I can't see the *logic* of her plan, but what can I say? I've messed up her life enough.

5

10

15

---

prejudice ['predʒədɪs] an unfair dislike of people who are different from you in colour, religion, beliefs etc.
logic ['lɒdʒɪk] way of thinking that seems correct and sensible

CHAPTER TEN

Monday morning. Sherry and I meet at the bus stop.

"You're still here?" I say with surprise.

"Mom says I can go to school for one last week," she says. Her eyes fill with *tears*. "I'm so unhappy."

5 "Me too."

She's treated me like crap, but it's hard to imagine life without her.

When the bus arrives, I leave Sherry in her new seat near the middle. Nick and Justin sit down next to me and start

10 giggling like a couple of girls. "What's so funny?" I ask.

"That was a good weekend," says Justin.

Nick laughs, but he has the sense to say nothing.

"What are you talking about?" I ask angrily.

"Shut up, Vinny," says Nick. "The whole bus doesn't

15 have to know."

"Why not tell everybody if you were so good this weekend?"

"Settle down," he says. "We got some. And you could have got some too."

20 Justin laughs and says, "Yeah, she would have given everybody some."

At the Indian bus stop I'm ready to fight them but I don't want Raedawn to hear what's going on. Steve gets on, followed by Charlie and his gang.

25 Charlie looks at me and shouts, "We were at the bridge waiting for you. Where were you?"

---

tear [tɪə] drop of water that comes out of your eye when you cry

I look away. The other Indians laugh. The door closes, but Raedawn is not on the bus. Where is she?

*

On Monday night Sherry comes round after supper. She looks terribly unhappy.

"What are we going to do?" she asks. "Mom and Aunt Stephanie are on the phone making arrangements for the weekend. Uncle Dick is coming on Saturday to take my things. Mom and Dad are going to pay them for looking after me. Can you imagine, Vinny? It's like I'm being sent to a *foster* home. For doing what? I've done nothing wrong. Have you talked to your parents yet?"

"I'll talk to them today. They'll talk to your parents. Maybe we can get them to change their minds."

"They are best friends," she says, and looks up at me hopefully. "What are you going to say?"

"I don't know. It depends what kind of mood they're in."

I have no idea what I will say to them. Mom and Dad are the last people in the world I want to talk to, and Steve and Sherry is the last subject I want to talk to them about. I already know what they think.

"They're upstairs now, Vinny. Go up and talk to them."

"Not now. I'll talk to them later."

"What good is later? Time is running out. Please…"

"Now?" I ask.

"Yeah, now – please. That will give your parents time to go over and talk to my parents. I'll stay down here and listen."

"No, you won't. If I'm going upstairs to talk to my

---

foster ['fɒstə] *home* family that looks after children who have problems with their parents, or no parents

parents, you're going home. You aren't listening to me!"

"Okay, okay," she says, looking disappointed. "You promise to come over and tell me what they said?"

"Yeah, I promise."

5 She gets up and leaves. I wonder why I promised to talk to them, but decide to go upstairs and say whatever comes into my head, depending on their *mood*. I know it's a stupid idea. They'll never be in the mood to hear what I'm going to say.

When I get upstairs, Dad is watching TV and Mom is 10 reading the newspaper.

"Mom," I begin. "Can I talk to you guys?"

Mom looks up. "Of course, *dear*. Jack, Vinny wants to talk to us. Can you turn the TV down?"

"Yeah, okay." He turns toward me. "What do you want?"

15 "Forget it," I say, and turn toward the stairs.

"No," Mom says. "We don't want to forget it. Jack, turn the TV down so we can hear."

Dad turns the *volume* down and says, "I'm listening."

He can hear me now, but I know he isn't going to listen 20 to a word I say.

"Sherry's going to move to town," I say. "Did you guys know that?"

"Yeah," Dad says. "So what?"

"So what?" I shout. "So what? It's her life. She's lived in 25 this village all her life. She's gone to school with all of us. She wants to graduate with her friends next year."

"She'll be *pregnant* before the year's out if she stays

---

mood [muːd] the way that you feel (happy, sad etc.)
dear [dɪə] word that is used to address somebody you like or love
volume [ˈvɒljuːm] amount of sound
pregnant [ˈpregnənt] expecting a baby

with that Indian *pothead*," he says. "At least this way she'll graduate somewhere."

"How can you say that?" I shout. "You're an idiot!"

"Vincent," Mom says, trying to control things. "Don't
5 shout at your father. Deb and Donnie are doing what they think is best for their daughter. It's none of our business."

"Oh, so now it's not your business," I say. "You've been on the phone day and night. I've heard you."

"We can't change their minds," says Mom *flatly*.
10 "But if you and Dad talk to them, won't they at least think again about what they're doing?"

"And what do you expect us to say?" laughs Dad. "Hey, Donnie, it's great that your daughter's hanging around with that Indian pothead! Good for her!"
15 "Vincent," Mom says, "we think it's a good idea for Sherry to move away." She *pauses*. "Before it's too late."

Dad turns back to the TV. "I'm not talking to Donnie. As soon as you told me about Sherry and that loser, I told Donnie to get his daughter out of this village fast."
20 I'm *furious*. I face Dad and shout, "You are a *dumbass*. Keep thinking like that and you'll lose one of your own kids, too."

I turn around and *rush* down the stairs.

"Vinny," Mom calls after me. "What do you mean?"

"What do you care what I mean!"
25 I slam the bedroom door. Sherry can wait until tomorrow to hear about my useless effort.

---

pothead ['pɒthed] impolite word for a person who uses the drug 'pot'
flat (here:) firm
to pause [pɔːz] to stop for a short time
furious ['fjʊəriəs] very angry
dumbass ['dʌmæs] stupid person
to rush [rʌʃ] to move quickly

"I was waiting for you to come over last night," Sherry says at the bus stop the next morning.

"Sorry, I was too annoyed to talk. Mom and Dad are no help. In fact they're worse than your parents."

I don't tell her that it was my dad's idea for her to move. 5

"So what are we going to do?" she asks. "How am I going to keep it from Steve?"

"You'd better tell him right away," I say as the bus pulls up, "before he hears it from someone else."

At the next stop, Steve gets on. As soon as he sits down, 10
Sherry *bursts* into tears as she tells him the bad news. I look for Raedawn, but she's not on the bus.

"What did you do to her?" I snap at Nick.

"We told you, man," he says as he looks round the bus.

"She's not here," I say. "She wasn't on the bus yesterday 15
either, man. She never misses school."

"What of it, man?" says Nick. "So she's not at school. What's that got to do with us?"

"That's the question," I say. "What's that got to do with you two?" 20

"She wanted us. I'm telling you the truth. Then she pulled away."

"What do you mean 'she pulled away'?"

"Well, after we got started, she gets all *moral* on us and

---

to burst [bɜːst] – *burst* – *burst* to break with great force
moral [ˈmɒrəl] having a strong feeling for the difference between good and bad

---

49

pushes us away. But not very hard," he says after a pause.

"What did she say?"

Nick isn't looking at me when he says, "She just shouted at us, man. So we took it anyway."

5 He's *lying*. But I can't tell which part is the lie. Raedawn's not coming to school, I'm sure about that. And Nick and Justin did something to her. But I know that Nick's not happy with his story.

"She was good, man," says Justin with a smile. "And she 10 liked it. She really liked it."

"Shut up man," I say. I've had enough.

*

Knock, knock, knock.

I look at my clock. It's 9:00 Tuesday night.

"Who is it?"

15 "Open the door," shouts Dad. "Right now!"

"All right, all right," I unlock the door. "What's your panic?"

Dad and Donnie burst into the room like a couple of *firemen*. "Where is she?" asks Donnie.

20 I ask, "Are you looking for Sherry?"

"Don't *play dumb*, Vince," says Dad.

Donnie says, "She didn't come home from school. Me and Deb were at the Raven's Eye having a few drinks with the guys after work. We got home half an hour ago. 25 Sherry's not home. No sign of her."

---

to lie [laɪ] – *lied* to not tell the truth
fireman person who fights fires
to play dumb [dʌm] to pretend that you don't know what is happening

I think to myself: 'Maybe you should have been looking for your daughter three hours ago.'

"She's probably at Meagan's house," I say.

"Deb's phoned all Sherry's girlfriends," says Dad.

"I'm going home to get my *gun*," says Donnie angrily. "You coming with me, Jack? I'm going down to the Indian reserve. I'll find her there." 5

"Hold on, Donnie," I say. "You don't need a gun. And you're in no condition to be going anywhere."

"I'm Sherry's father…" He sounds drunk. 10

"Donnie," Dad interrupts. *Luckily* he hasn't had so much to drink as Donnie. He can see there may be trouble if he can't stop his friend. "We'll find her."

"I'll go to the reserve and look for her," I say.

"That's great, Vince," says Dad. "Let's you and me go back to your house, Donnie. Vince will find Sherry. She's probably with Steve." 15

"Let me at that son of a bitch!" shouts Donnie, almost falling over.

"Let Vince get Sherry back first," says Dad. "Deal with the pothead later." 20

Dad looks pleased that we're agreeing with each other, and Donnie's happy with Dad's plan. They walk out and leave me. So I'm going to the reserve to find Sherry, am I? Chicken Legs is going to walk straight into the middle of the reserve and stand up to Charlie? I'm going to get killed! I've never been on the reserve before. I don't know anyone 25

---

lucky ['lʌki] having good fortune

gun [gʌn]

4*

who lives there. I don't know where Steve lives. Charlie and his friends might be there. I might run into Raedawn. This is all I need. I put on my jacket and shoes and go out into the night. The moon is so bright that I can see almost as well
5 as in daylight. The cold air *stings* my *lungs*, but I'm thinking about Raedawn and what I can say to her: 'I'm sorry for what my friends did. I'm not like them. Really, I'm not.'

I cross the bridge and walk down the *avenue* of old trees that leads to the reserve. Usually, I love the forest, but
10 tonight I get a strange feeling that the sooner I get out the better.

I reach the old sign that says: Indian Reserve. No *Trespassing*. I've never imagined walking past the sign and down the road – alone. I can't go back. Raedawn might be
15 there. Before I have time to think too hard, I turn onto the reserve. I walk in the *shadow* of the trees until I reach a clearing. Suddenly I can see three roads and at least twenty or thirty houses.

Okay. What did I expect? A sign that said 'Steve, This
20 Way'? How am I going to find him?

I walk down the first road to my right. There's a bunch of teenagers on the *porch* of a house up ahead. Before I can think what to do, a girl shouts, "Hey, white boy. You lost?"

"No," I shout back. "Or maybe, yes."
25 Someone switches a light on and they all start laughing.

---

to sting – stung [stʌŋ] – *stung* to hurt with short, sharp pain
lung [lʌŋ] organ of the body into which we breathe air
avenue ['ævɪnjuː] straight double row of trees with a road in the middle
to trespass ['trespəs] to go onto land where you are not allowed
shadow ['ʃædəʊ] see vignette on page 12
porch [pɔːtʃ] small platform with a roof in front of a door

"It's Chicken Legs. You were supposed to meet Charlie last Friday, under the bridge. You're late!"

I can't see Charlie, but I recognize some of his friends and the girls, of course. As the noise gets louder, more porch lights come on. I wonder which house is Raedawn's. 5

"I'm Richie, man. What do you want?" A guy comes down the stairs and meets me on the road.

"I'm Vince, and I'm looking for Sherry," I say. "She didn't get home from school and her dad's *going nuts*."

"We know who you are," he says. He turns round to the 10 others on the porch. "Anyone see Sherry after school?"

Nobody has seen her, but a girl says, "I'm Lucy. Go see Steve. He'll know where Sherry is."

"Can you tell me where he lives?"

Lucy points down the road on the other side. Richie 15 leads the way. The rest of the crowd follows.

"So Steve's got himself a lady," Richie says. "Let's go find her."

"He's going to get into trouble," says Lucy. "He should just leave her alone. He doesn't need this." 20

Richie steps up to the front door of a bright yellow house. Even in the dark the place looks like a sunflower. He rings the bell and then stands back.

A huge woman with a lot of thick hair looks out from an upstairs window. 25

"You looking for Steve?" she asks.

"Yeah," says Richie. "This guy's here to talk to him."

She turns round, shouts, "Steve!" and then disappears.

Steve appears at the door.

---

to go nuts [nʌts] to get very angry

"What's going on?" he asks when he sees me. "Is Sherry okay?"

"No, man," I say. "I'm looking for her. Don't you know where she is?"

5 "Why should I? Last time I saw her she was on the bus."

"She didn't get home from school."

"No way, man. Then where is she?"

"I was hoping you could tell me."

He goes upstairs and comes back wearing his jacket.

10 "I'll find her," he says, and gets into a car beside the house. He races off and leaves me standing on the porch. What do I do next?

Richie says, "We'll check down at the beach for you, man. Sometimes white chicks *chill out* down there."

15 "Thanks," I say. "I'll check with her friends."

"You can find your way home?" asks Richie.

"Yeah, no problem." I walk up the road as if I know exactly where I'm going. Richie and the others stay behind discussing what to do in the middle of the road.

20 I walk slowly, looking at each house for signs of Raedawn. Every house has the same windows, same porch and same driveway. Through some of the windows I can see TVs, lights, *fridges, stoves* – no different from our side of the village. A girl walks toward me on the other side of the road.

25 She looks a bit like Raedawn, but I soon see it isn't her.

"Hi," I say, but she looks away and ignores me.

---

to chill [tʃɪl] *out* to relax
fridge electric device for keeping food cool
stove [stəʊv] device for heating and cooking food

I'm feeling more *confident* now, and instead of going
straight back home I turn into a short side street. All the
lights are out in the second house on the right except the
porch light, and I see a girl sitting in a big chair on the
porch. I'm sure it's Raedawn.   5

I slow down and start thinking of something to say when
it suddenly begins to *rain*. I forget my words and just wave
as I pass her house. She doesn't move, but I can feel her eyes
on me. I just manage to say "Hi" as I walk past her.

When I finally turn onto the main street, the words   10
come.

"I'm not one of them, Raedawn. Really I'm not. I'm sorry
for what they did."

"What did you say?" It's the voice of an old man who
comes out of the *darkness* wearing a   15
plastic rain jacket and hat. He
stops in front of me.

"Nothing. I was just talking to
myself."

"Let me tell you something,   20
son. If you're sorry for
something then pick up the *bat*,
step up to the *plate* and play
the ball. It ain't going to
do you no good walking   25

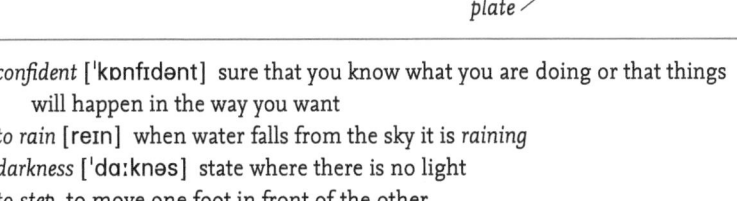

bat

plate

---

confident ['kɒnfɪdənt] sure that you know what you are doing or that things
    will happen in the way you want
to rain [reɪn] when water falls from the sky it is *raining*
darkness ['dɑːknəs] state where there is no light
to step to move one foot in front of the other

down a dark road in the rain talking to yourself for the rest of your life."

He walks on past me. By the time I turn round, he's gone. My heart is beating fast.

5 'Step up to the plate. Pick up the bat. Play the ball.' I'm a *drowned rat*, standing in the road, waving my hands and shouting like a *lunatic*.

For a moment I'm not afraid. I'm ready to run back to Raedawn's house and tell her everything. Then the feeling 10 goes away and I race through the bushes to the bridge without stopping.

---

to drown [draʊn] to die in deep water because you cannot swim
rat animal like a large mouse
lunatic [ˈluːnətɪk] mad person

CHAPTER TWELVE

Just past the gas station a car pulls over in front of me.

Steve *sticks* his head out of the window. "Jump in."

"It's okay, man. I'm *wet* through. I'll walk home."

Then I see Sherry leaning against him, crying. I get into the back of the car.   5

"She's afraid to go home," Steve says.

"Vince," *sobs* Sherry. "Steve wants to talk to Mom and Dad. There's no way. Tell him it's a bad idea."

"It's a good idea," I say. What *harm* can it do? Donnie and Deb are going to send Sherry away anyway.   10

"Vince!" she cries. "They'll kill me."

"No they won't. They'll send you to town to live with your aunt. They were going to do that anyway."

"You're no help at all!"

"Yeah, I know. Don't *rub it in*."   15

"Thanks, buddy," says Steve. "Maybe they won't hate me so much if they meet me."

"Don't count on it," I say. "But it can't make matters worse."

"You guys don't know my parents," sobs Sherry.

"Yes I do," I say. "There's a good chance that this won't   20
help. But nothing else has helped. Any better ideas?"

---

to stick out – stuck [stʌk] *– stuck (here:)* to push outwards
wet covered in water
to sob [sɒb] to make a sound by breathing in when crying
harm damage
to rub [rʌb] *something in* to remind somebody frequently of something they
    may want to forget

"No. Will you come in with us then?"

"Why not?" I say.

Donnie and Deb look shocked when they open the door.
Steve has his arm around Sherry. I'm standing behind
them. Before they get over their shock, Steve steps forward 5
and holds out his hand to Donnie.

"My name is Steve," he says. "I found Sherry near the river."

When Steve lets go of Donnie's hand, it falls to his side.
Donnie's mouth is open but no words come out. Steve
gives Sherry a *nudge* as if it's her turn to speak. 10

"I'm sorry if you were worried about me," she says in a
kind of *stubborn monotone*.

Still Deb and Donnie say nothing.

"Mr. Porter," Steve says. He steps closer and looks
Donnie in the eye. "I'm sorry for any trouble I've caused 15
your family, but Sherry and I like each other. I don't want
our relationship to get in the way of her family or her
education. But I don't want to stop seeing her either."

Donnie's too confused to say anything. Then Steve turns
to Deb. He takes her hand and says, "Sherry won't *scare* you 20
again, Mrs. Porter. Not if I can help it."

Sherry's looking as confused as her parents – as me.
Steve's totally in charge – the only one out of the five of us
with his feet on the ground. I watch in *amazement* as he
steps up to the plate and plays the ball. Donnie and Deb start 25

---

to nudge [nʌdʒ] to touch a person with your elbow to remind him or her to do
   something
stubborn [ˈstʌbən] not willing to change your mind
monotone [ˈmɒnətəʊn] sound which stays at the same level all the time
to scare [skeə] to shock or frighten
amazement [əˈmeɪzmənt] very strong surprise or shock

5*

nodding at him as if maybe they don't hate Indians after all.

"That's what we're worried about," Donnie says. "We don't want Sherry *missing school* and spending all her time with a boy."

5   "Of course, Mr. Porter," Steve says.

"I was so worried," Deb says.

Steve gives Sherry another nudge.

She says, "I'm sorry, Mom," sounding as *unconvincing* as she did the first time.

10   Deb gives her a hug. Donnie shakes Steve's hand without thinking about it. I walk home. In a few minutes I hear Steve's car *roaring* down the road.

*

In the morning, Sherry's waiting for me at the bus stop.

"Thanks, Vince," she says.

15   "For what?"

"For getting Steve last night. And for being there."

"Yeah, no problem. How's it going?"

"Mom and Dad were angry with me after Steve left. But at least they *blame* me for everything, not him. By the time

20 Mom was finished with me, it sounded as if she thought I was a bad *influence* on Steve!"

---

to nod to move your head up and down to say 'yes'
to miss school to not go to school
unconvincing [ˌʌnkənˈvɪnsɪŋ] not able to make somebody believe that
    something is true
to roar [rɔː] to make a loud, angry noise like a lion, tiger etc.
to blame somebody to say that somebody is responsible for something bad that
    happens
influence [ˈɪnfluəns] power to affect another person's actions, behaviour etc.

"Maybe you are."

She punches my arm.

"I'm grounded for a month because I scared them so much. But I don't have to move away. And I'm only allowed to see Steve at school. I can live with that."   5

"Or get around it," I add.

Sherry laughs.

"Sherry," I say. Then I *hesitate*. Pick up the bat, you moron. "Sherry," I say again in case she didn't hear me.

"Yeah?"   10

"Sherry."

"Vince, Vince, Vince." She's laughing at me! "You got something stuck in your *throat*?"

"Yeah. It's been stuck there for weeks."

"Then *spit* it out."   15

So I tell her. Everything. In ten minutes she knows the whole story. I tell her stuff I didn't even know myself. I tell her about Nick and Justin. I tell her how Raedawn looked at me and how it feels when she says my name. I tell her I can't think of anything else but Raedawn. I tell her that   20 Raedawn ignored me last night.

The bus arrives before Sherry can say anything. She puts her arms around me and gives me a big hug.

"*Geez*, Vinny, I would never have *guessed*. Leave it with me. I'll take care of it."   25

---

to hesitate ['hezɪteɪt] to pause for a moment because you are unsure
throat [θrəʊt] your *throat* is between your mouth and your stomach
to spit – spat – spat to push something out of your mouth with great force
Geez [dʒiːz] *(slang:)* word – short for 'Jesus' – used to express surprise
to guess [ges] *(here:)* to realize that something is true

I jump onto the bus as light as a *feather*. A ten-minute talk has lifted a *ton* of concrete off my shoulders.

★

Coach Baker is going to be happy with me today. Mr. Basketball has returned. At lunch I race down to the gym. 5 When I pass the office I see a police car stopping outside. A car full of old Indians stops behind it, followed by a woman in a *pickup* with Raedawn sitting beside her.

I'm going to be late for basketball practice, but I want to know what's going on. A crowd *gathers* outside the office.

10 "We're meeting with *Principal* Chatterton," says the police officer.

"Then we'll find the boys and talk to them," an old

feather [ˈfeðə] birds are covered in *feathers*
ton [tʌn] unit of weight (over 1000 kilos)
pickup [ˈpɪkʌp] small truck with low sides
to gather [ˈgæðə] to come together
principal [ˈprɪnsɪpl] head teacher at an American or Canadian school

Indian woman says. "We will sit together and hear what they have to say."

For a moment I think I should tell Nick and Justin what's going on. Then I think, 'Why protect them?' This is Raedawn's game. She doesn't need me. When the group goes into the principal's office, I run for the gym.

"Vince," Coach Baker *yells*. "You're late!"

"Yeah, Coach. But I'm all here."

I play well. I feel good. Coach Baker is happy with me.

Yeah – I feel good. Sherry's not moving away, we're friends again, she knows about Raedawn, and my two former best friends will get what they deserve.

Suddenly I hear my name on the *PA system*.

"Vince Hardy to the office."

"What now?" Coach Baker yells. "Don't be long!"

"No, sir," I say.

*

Mrs. Chatterton's waiting at the office door with two police officers and an old Indian lady. There's no sign of Raedawn.

"Vince, do you know where Nick and Justin are?" asks Mrs. Chatterton *sternly*.

"No," I say.

She looks at me as if she thinks I'm lying.

"When did you last see them?"

---

to yell [jel] to scream with anger or pain

PA (= public address) system system to pass messages to large groups of people through a number of loudspeakers

stern [stɜːn] strict; serious

"In math class."

"And you haven't seen them during lunch?"

"I've been at basketball practice. Nick and Justin didn't come."

5 "Why not?" she asks.

"How should I know?" I reply.

"Vince," she says firmly. "I'll ask you again. Where are Nick and Justin?"

"I don't know." They must have seen the police and run.
10 Even she should be able to work that out.

The old Indian woman looks at me as if she could tell me exactly how much money I've got in my pockets. "Young man. Do you know why we're looking for Nick and Justin?"

15 I look her straight in the eye and lie. "No, *ma'am*."

The old lady shakes her head. She says slowly, "We'll talk to this young man later."

"You can go, Vince," says Mrs. Chatterton. "We'll call you when we need you."

20 Lunch is almost over. I run out to the parking lot to look for the pickup which Raedawn arrived in. Gone.

*

Nick and Justin aren't on the bus after school. Neither is Raedawn. Steve and Sherry haven't showed up yet. I sit down on the empty seat in front of Dune. I turn round and
25 say, "Hey, man. How's it going?"

---

ma'am [mæm] (= *madam*) polite form of address for a woman

"Good. You?" he answers.

"Yeah. I'm good, too." We're talking like old friends.

I know it's just a bus seat, but all of a sudden it's a whole new thing. I'm sitting at the front of the bus, and it's *weird*. The Indian kids start filling up the seats around me. Richie sits next to me.

Looking like there's never been a seating arrangement, he says, "You guys find Sherry the other night?"

"Yeah," I say. "Thanks."

When Dune gets off the bus, Sherry and Steve move up behind me and I tell them and Richie what happened at lunch – the police, the old lady, Raedawn. Everything.

When I finish my story, Steve says, "Go down to the beach tonight, Vince. Wait at the *campsite* office around seven."

---

weird [ˈwɪəd] very strange
campsite place where tourists can camp

It's still raining that night, so I put on a plastic rain jacket and hat and pull on my *rubber boots*. I look like an idiot.

Walking down the road, I try to work out what Steve is planning. He seems to have things under control.

5 It is dark outside. The river is very full.

I walk across the bridge, over the hill and down to the campsite office. I walk through *puddles* the size of small swimming pools.

"Steve!" But nobody could hear me above the noise of
10 the sea, the river, the rain and the wind in the trees. I walk up the steps to the porch of the campsite office.

"Steve!" I call, shaking myself like a wet dog.

I can't see or hear anyone. I turn round and see what looks like someone lying by my feet.

15 "Steve?"

What is he doing? I *bend* down and find myself face to face with Raedawn.

"Hey! Where's Steve?"

"I don't know."

20 Her voice grabs me like an electric shock. You know what happens when you have planned exactly what to do in a certain situation: when it happens you forget everything.

---

rubber boot [ˌrʌbəˈbuːt] high shoe made of the waterproof material *rubber*
puddle [ˈpʌdl] pool of rainwater
to bend down – bent – bent to move your head and the top of your body
    towards the ground

I'm finally alone with Raedawn and I'm *paralyzed*.

"What are you doing here?" I ask.

"What are you doing here?"

"Steve told me to come to the campsite office."

"He told me to come here as well," she says.   5

"Why?" I ask.

"I don't know."

"It doesn't look like he's going to show," she says,
getting up. "I think I'll go home."

I stand up, too. She's like a *magnet*. I look out to sea, but   10
I feel her staring at me. she's less than two feet away and
looking straight up at me. Finally she looks away and I take
a quick look at her.

"Don't go home," I say.

I grab a corner of her jacket. She jumps away.   15

"Let go of me!"

I back up a few steps.

"Sorry," I say. "I'm really sorry. I just don't want you to go."

"Why not?"

"I want to talk to you."   20

"You mean you want to lie to me."

"Why do you say that?"

"You lied to my grandmother today. You said you
didn't know why they were looking for your two *disgusting*
friends."   25

"I'm sorry. I really am sorry."

---

to paralyze ['pærəlaız] to make a person or animal unable to move

magnet ['mæɡnət] piece of metal with an electrical charge that can pull
certain metals towards it

disgusting [dɪz'ɡʌstɪŋ] making you feel physically sick

She leans against the wall. We both wait for the other to
speak.

I speak first. "Are you all right, Raedawn?" I'm not sure,
but it feels like I'm picking up the bat. "I want you to be all
5 right."

"Yeah, well how will I be all right with guys like you and
your friends around?"

"I'm not like my friends."

"Yeah, right, Vince. I've lived around here for as long
10 as you. You and those two *creeps* are like *triplets*. Seen one,
seen them all."

"No, Raedawn," I *protest*.

"I thought I liked you before Friday. Then it happened."

"What happened?" I ask.

15 "What do you mean? Didn't your friends tell you?"

"Yeah, but I don't know if it's true. I can't believe it."

"You can't believe it!?" she cries. She sounds very angry. "You can't believe your friends would *attack* me? That
they would hold me down on the ground and try to *rip* my
20 clothes off? You can't believe they would call me a *slut*?
What is there about that that you can't understand?"

"Then you didn't want them? And they didn't have sex
with you? And you didn't tell them that you liked it?"

"What? What did you say? What did they tell you?"

---

creep [kriːp] very unpleasant person
triplets [ˈtrɪpləts] three children born at the same time from the same mother
to protest [prəˈtest] to say that you strongly disagree with what somebody says
to attack [əˈtæk] to use force against a person
to rip to pull something with enough force to break or tear it
slut [slʌt] woman with no sexual morals

I throw my arms around her and this time she doesn't pull away. She holds me close and starts to cry.

"They said that about me? That's what you think happened?"

"No. That's why I wanted to talk to you."

"Do you believe me?"

I hold her *tight* and can feel her heavy sobs against the beating of my own heart.

"Yeah, I believe you. Their story didn't make sense right from the start. But I didn't know the real story. I didn't want to believe them."

I hide my face in her thick black hair. I feel a *cramp* in the back of my *neck*, but I don't move. I don't want this moment to end. She stays perfectly still, too. She may be thinking the same thing. Seconds turn into minutes. After a while I get a weird feeling that I'm standing on solid ground for the first time in my life. I feel like I'm Vince Hardy and don't have to be afraid or *embarrassed* any more. This must be how Steve felt when he met Sherry's parents. When I feel that I can *handle* my new feeling, I *squeeze* Raedawn a little to test the water. She moves closer. I *nuzzle* my face in her hair.

---

tight [taɪt] opposite of 'loose'

cramp [kræmp] tight feeling in a muscle

neck part of your body on which your head rests

embarrassed [ɪmˈbærəst] feeling nervous before or after making a silly
    mistake

to handle to use properly

to squeeze [skwiːz] to press together hard

to nuzzle [ˈnʌzl] to push your face against part of another person's body

This is home, man. This is where I belong.

For a moment I think of Mom and Dad. I can see myself standing at the front door with my arm around Raedawn.

"Dad and Mom," I would say. "I'd like you to meet Raedawn." 5

I can't see their reaction in my thoughts, but that doesn't matter. I've picked up the bat and hit the ball. I'm in the game and I'm ready to play each ball as it comes.

"My Mom's not going to be very happy when I bring a white boy home," Raedawn says. 10

I laugh. "You must be *kidding*. I was just thinking the same thing about my parents."

---

to kid to joke

Comprehension and activities

Comprehension
1. What do you find out about the narrator of the story in this chapter?
2. What impression do you get of the place and the people who live there?
3. In what way is Dune different from the other kids?
4. In what ways has the village changed over the last ten or twenty years?
5. Explain the differences in the attitudes of the narrator's parents.

Activities
1. Where do you live? Compare the place where you live with the village in the story.
2. Are you happy living where you live? If not, describe your 'dream location'.
3. In North America, the word 'city' often means no more than 'town', but in Britain there is a difference in the way the two words are used. Find out what it is. And what does 'the City' with a capital C refer to in British English?

Give your own opinion
What do you understand by the term 'First Nations'?

CHAPTER ONE

Comprehension
1. Where you live, are there many people who – or whose parents – come from a different country? Say something about them.
2. Are there any problems between local people and these immigrants?
3. What has happened to Sherry during the summer?
4. In what way is the word 'hot' used in connection with Sherry?
5. How have the feelings of the narrator – whose name we still

do not know – changed towards Sherry?
6. Why doesn't the narrator hit Steve or beat him up?

Activities
1. How tall is 'six three' in metric? How heavy are 'forty or fifty pounds'? Find out something about the old British and American system of weights and measures known as 'avoir-dupois' on the Internet.
2. What do you know about rugby? Where was the game invented? What sort of a game is it? In which countries is it played? Which country is the current world champion? Find out as many facts as you can.

Give your own opinion
What is the main difference between the situation with immigrants in your country and in Canada or the USA?

CHAPTER TWO

Comprehension
1. What is Sherry's attitude towards Vince in this chapter? Quote one or two of the things she says to him that express her new attitude.
2. What are the reasons for the change in Vince's attitude towards Sherry?
3. Why does Vince call his friends 'wimps'?
4. What does the Indian girl mean when she says "It happens" to Vince?

Activities
1. Summarize what happens in this short chapter in a few sentences.
2. Sport is quite important at schools in the USA and Canada. Which two sports have already been mentioned in the story? Are they both equally popular in both countries?
3. Talk about the behaviour of Vince and Steve in connection with Sherry. How does it differ?

Chapter Three

Comprehension

1. Why is the basketball team no good this year?
2. What happens to Vince in the gym and how does it affect his playing?
3. What does the word 'Chicken!' mean when it is used of a person?
4. What does Vince think about himself at the end of this chapter?
5. Which developments in the previous chapter have led to Vince's personality crisis?

Activities

1. Talk (or write) about the sports that are popular at your school or in your country. Is basketball one of them?
2. Which sport or sports do you play – or did you play – at school?
3. Do you worry about what other people say or think about you?

Chapter Four

Comprehension

1. Why is Vince terrified in this chapter?
2. What change in Vince's attitude towards Indians do you notice in this chapter?
3. What can you say about the two boys Manny and Turner?
4. What differences are there in the attitudes of Vince and Justin towards Raedawn?
5. What do you think is happening to Vince?

Activities

1. The bus trip to and from school takes three hours each day. How do you think the kids spend this time? What would you do with these three hours?
2. Bussing kids to town schools from distant villages is time-consuming and expensive. What alternatives can you think of?

Chapter Five

Comprehension

1. How does Vince's mom know about what happened on the bus?

2. Why doesn't Vince want to talk about what happened?
3. Why does Vince's dad get so angry?
4. What happens on the bus the next morning?

Activities
What can you say about the people in the story so far? What sort of people are they? Write a couple of sentences about Vince, his mother, his father and Sherry. Give as many positive and negative characteristics as you can.

Give your own opinion
1. Where do you think Ronny has gone to live and why? Give reasons for your opinion.
2. Steve was voted the most popular guy in the school. What does this tell you about the attitude towards Indians in other parts of Canada?

CHAPTER SIX

Comprehension
1. What differences do you notice in the way Vince is treated by Steve and by Charlie?
2. 'That's not all that's changed' says Vince to himself in this chapter. How many things have changed for him and why are these changes important?
3. 'They play rugby – we play basketball'. What does this mean in the context of fighting?
4. What reasons does Vince give for not going to the bridge?
5. Nick and Justin have gone to meet the Indians at the bridge. What do you think will happen next?

Activities
1. Do you enjoy playing video games? Give your reasons.
2. If you are working in a group, discuss your favourite video games.
3. Discuss what you would do in this situation if you were Vince.

Give your own opinion

1. 'I feel sorry for Steve. He's got himself into a hell of a mess.' What do you think Vince means – and do you agree with him?
2. At the end of this chapter, Vince says to himself: 'I realize that I used to be that stupid'. What do you think he means?

CHAPTER SEVEN

Comprehension

1. Why do Justin and Nick find it difficult to 'tell the story' of what happened that night?
2. Do you think that Vince and his family are deeply religious people? If not, how do you explain Vince's disappointment about not having 'some time with God'.
3. Why doesn't Vince go upstairs and talk to his parents about his problems?

Activities

1. Without reading this chapter again, write down a short summary of what happens.
2. How much do we know about Vince's family? Write down any information you can remember about his father and mother, the family situation etc.

Give your own opinion

1. Do you think that Vince was a coward not to face the Indians?
2. Would you be able to talk to people if you had a problem like Vince's? Which people would you talk to?

CHAPTER EIGHT

Comprehension

1. What 'doesn't often happen' in the Hardy household, and what does this tell you about the family?
2. Why has Sherry lied to her parents about who she was with the previous night?

3. Why is Vince suddenly on Sherry's side at the end of the chapter?
4. What impression do you get of Indians in this chapter? Do you believe it is true? Give your reasons.

Give your own opinion

Do you believe that there is any connection between the amount of time which people spend watching TV and their intelligence? If you are working in a group, tell the others about your own TV-watching habits – and enjoy a lively discussion!

CHAPTER NINE

Comprehension

1. In what way have Vince's feelings towards Sherry changed since the start of the story?
2. Why does Vince think that Sherry's problems are his fault?
3. In what way does Sherry's description of Steve differ from the normal prejudiced view of Indians?
4. What arguments do you think Vince could use to convince his and Sherry's parents not to send Sherry away?

Activities

1. The author of this story married an Indian at the age of 17 and brought up her four children on a First Nations reserve. Discuss how this qualifies her to write about prejudice.
2. If you are working in a group, discuss any prejudices which exist in your own society. Is prejudice ever justified?

CHAPTER TEN

Comprehension

1. Why do you think that Raedawn isn't on the school bus today?
2. Do you think that the fact that Raedawn isn't going to school confirms what Justin and Nick have told Vince?
3. Why is it difficult for Vince to talk to his father about serious matters?
4. What does Vince mean when he says "Keep thinking like that and you'll lose one of your own kids, too" at the end of this chapter?

Activities

1. What do you understand by the term 'generation gap'? Talk – or write – about your own experiences with this feature of modern life.
2. Do you think that you could have handled the situation in a better way? If you are working in a group, you can organize a discussion – or several discussions if your group is big enough – between Vince and his parents.

Give your own opinion

What is the main thing that worries Vince's parents about Sherry's relationship with Steve?

CHAPTER ELEVEN

Comprehension

1. Vince thinks that Nick is lying about what he and Justin did to Raedawn. 'But I can't tell which part is the lie,' he says to himself. Which part do you think is the lie?
2. Why is Vince so afraid about going to the Indian reserve?
3. How is Vince treated by the Indians on the reserve?
4. Do you think that the girl Vince saw really was Raedawn? Does it matter?
5. What advice does the old Indian give to Vince? What does it mean?

Activities

What sort of gun do you think Donnie has? In what ways do gun politics differ in Canada and the USA, where there is a very strong 'gun lobby'? Look up 'Gun politics' or 'Right to bear arms' on the Internet and find out. Now compare what you have found with the law in your own country?

Give your own opinion

1. What impression do you get of Sherry's father in this chapter?
2. If Sherry is not with Steve, where else could she be?

CHAPTER TWELVE

Comprehension

1. Where did Steve find Sherry?
2. Why was she there?
3. How does Steve handle the situation?
4. Why are Donnie and Deb so shocked?
5. In what way has Vince stepped up to the plate in this chapter?
6. What does Sherry mean when she says "Leave it with me. I'll take care of it" to Vince at the bus stop?
7. Why doesn't Vince sit at the back of the bus on the way home?

Activities

1. Which event in connection with bus-seating arrangements in the USA in the 1950s marked the start of the victory of the Civil Rights movement? If you have trouble finding information, just type James F. Blake or Rosa Parks into your Internet browser and look at the Wikipedia articles on these people. In what way were the seating arrangements different from those on the Canadian school bus in the story?
2. Think about race-related problems in other countries. Which ones have been solved, and how was this done? Which ones have not yet been solved, and how do you think they could be?

Give your own opinion

Why do you think the police have come to the school?

CHAPTER THIRTEEN

Comprehension

1. What connection is there between the weather and the mood of the story at the start of this chapter?
2. Who has arranged the meeting between Vince and Raedawn?
3. Why does Raedawn jump away from Vince when he touches her jacket?
4. Does Raedawn show prejudice in any way?
5. What is ironic about Raedawn's last comment in the story?

Activities

1. Prejudice is not based only on race or colour. Which other types of prejudice do you know about? Make a list of them, with examples. Would you consider the people in your country to be less prejudiced than people in other countries? Give your reasons and discuss if you are working in a group.
2. Did you remember to list the traditional prejudices of men towards women, which are only slowly disappearing even in some of the most progressive countries? Talk about them, too!
3. Vince says: 'For the first time in my life. I feel like I'm Vince Hardy and don't have to be afraid or embarrassed any more.' How do you think this feeling will help him to solve his other problems? (If you have forgotten what these problems are, look again at the beginning of Chapter Six.)

Give your own opinion

This story has a happy ending. But what about the lives of the two 'couples' if they stay together in the future? Work out a 'best-case' and a 'worst-case' scenario for Steve/Sherry and Vince/Raedawn and compare your notes with those of others who have read the story.

Whole-book project

Write an article for the Rocky View High School Magazine about what happens in the story. Make it as interesting as possible and put a lot of emphasis on the breaking down of prejudices.

Find more excercises on:
www.easyreaders.eu

Teen Reader Titles Now Available

ENGLISH

LEVEL 0
PHILIP HEWITT: Emma and the Boy Next Door (Sound)
ANN HALAM: The Shadow on the Stairs

LEVEL 1
PETER JOHNSON: Runaway Teacher
ALAN POSENER: The Double Life of a Very Black Cat
STEPHEN SPEIGHT: Bed & Breakfast (Sound)
STEPHEN SPEIGHT: The Runaway
JEREMY TAYLOR: Dr Schnitzler´s Dog
JEREMY TAYLOR: All 4 Love (Sound)
WOLF/FERRO: The Missing Mascot (Sound)

LEVEL 2
RITA BENNET: The Scary Chat Room (Sound)
KEVIN BROOKS: Johnny Delgado – Private Detective
ANNIE DALTON: Friday Forever
PAUL DAVENPORT: Horror Trip on the Pecos River (Sound)
JAMES HENEGHAN: Hit Squad
JAMES HENEGHAN & NORMA CHARLES: Bank Job
PHILIP HEWITT: Helping Hands
PHILIP HEWITT: Terror in the Hills
GEORGE IVANOFF: The Bookworm Mystery
KAREN MCCOMBIE: Love is the Drug
E. E. RICHARDSSON: Black Bones
E. E. RICHARDSSON: Devil for Sale (Sound)
STEPHEN SPEIGHT: The Fjord Murder (Sound)
STEPHEN SPEIGHT: Summer School Adventures
ANDY STANTON: Sterling and the Canary
JEREMY STRONG: Mad Iris
JEREMY TAYLOR: Football Friends (Sound)
JEREMY TAYLOR: Luke (Sound)
LEE WEATHERLY: Them

LEVEL 3
ANNE CASSIDY: Talking to Strangers
PAUL DAVENPORT: A Matter of Principle
PAUL DAVENPORT: Crossroads to Love (Sound)
PAUL DAVENPORT: Wolf Watch
PAUL DAVENPORT: Snakeman
CHARLES FERRO: Horror at Remsen High
CHARLES FERRO: Moonstruck
CHARLES FERRO: Love Ties
CHARLES FERRO: Burning Love
CHARLES FERRO: The Fortune Teller
CHARLES FERRO: Kool-1
CHARLES FERRO: The Cave Mystery
CHARLES FERRO: Vampire Skeletons
CHARLES FERRO: Voodoo Zombies
PHILIP HEWITT: Quest for a Father
SYLVIA OLSEN: Yellow Line
ALAN POSENER: Oh! Carol and Other Steve Stories
JEREMY TAYLOR: Love me Blindly
TONY VARRATO: Fakie

LEVEL 4
CHARLES FERRO: Forever Young
CHARLES FERRO: Over the Line
HOLLY-JANE RAHLENS: One Fine Day

GERMAN

LEVEL 0
IRIS FELTER: Mädchen & Der Junge am Meer (Sound)
GRETA GALLANDY: Keine Angst? (Sound)
PATRICIA MENNEN: Kopftuch

LEVEL 1
IRIS FELTER: Tanz mit mir!
GRETA GALLANDY: Im Chatroom gefangen
ALAN POSENER: Kater, Ines und Katerina

Level 2
ALAN POSENER: Märchenland
ELSEGRET RUGE: Vier Freunde - Abenteuer in München (Sou

LEVEL 3
ALAN POSENER: Olli aus Ossiland

FRENCH

LEVEL 0
LAURENT JOUVET: Radio mystère (Sound)
CHRISTIANE STÉFANOPOLI:
   Catastrophe au Camping des Roses (Sound)

LEVEL 1
MICHEL AMELIN: Cent vingt minutes pour mourir
PASCAL GARNIER: Les enfants de la nuit (Sound)
LENIA MAJOR: La lettre mystérieuse
BRIGITTE PESKINE: Mon grand petit frère (Sound)
JÉRÔME TALOU: Parce que je t'aime

LEVEL 2
STÉPHANE DANIEL: Un agent trés secret
ANNA GAVALDA: 35 kilo d'espoir
CHARLOTTE GINGRAS: Un été de Jade
LAURENT JOUVET: Anne et l'ordinateur (Sound)
LAURENT JOUVET: Répétition pour un crime
JÉRÔME TALOU: L'amour par internet (Sound)
PAUL THIÈS: Un automne rouge sang (Sound)

LEVEL 3
MICHAËL OLLIVIER: Frères de sang
JÉRÔME TALOU: Bruno et l'amour

LEVEL 4
HALLUM/LOUVEAU: Choc des cultures

SPANISH

LEVEL 0
JAIME CORPAS: Amigos virtuales
JAVIER NAVARRO: Un mundo fantástico

LEVEL 1
JAIME CORPAS: Misterio en la Sagrada Familia
JAVIER NAVARRO: Una historia de montaña

LEVEL 2
JAVIER NAVARRO: Las estátuas de Machu Picchu

Sound: Available as either Mp3 or CD,
check www.easyreaders.eu

Teen Reader Titles Now Available

Read On Series
English
Level 2 (A2) - including CD
BENNI BØDKER: Sarin in Sulphur Valley
BENNI BØDKER: Sarin in the Emperor's City
BENNI BØDKER: Sarin in the Foggy Mountains
BENNI BØDKER: Sarin in Nordheim
BENNI BØDKER: Sarin in the Salt Mine
BENNI BØDKER: Sarin and the star Tower

A-team Series
– Free mp3 available at WWW.EASYREADERS.EU
Level 3
DANIEL ZIMAKOFF & IDA-MARIE RENDTORFF: The Computer Mystery
DANIEL ZIMAKOFF & IDA-MARIE RENDTORFF: The Stolen Monkey
DANIEL ZIMAKOFF & IDA-MARIE RENDTORFF: Kidnapped

Labyrinth Series
German
Level 3 (A2/B1)
MARTINA GATTERMANN: Ein dramatischer Urlaub
    (Sound available)
MARTINA GATTERMANN: SOS aus Wien
    (Sound available)
MARTINA GATTERMANN: Horror in Hintertux
MARTINA GATTERMANN: Abenteuer in Berlin